I0618079

*Dedication*

*To the ultimate Creator, Author and
Perfecter of my life and faith, amen.*

*To my family and friends,
I love you and thank you.*

*If you were gifted this book, the brave and daring human is trying to tell you one of two things: they see you, or they want to be seen.*

*If you gifted this book to yourself, you want to see people in this life more abundantly.*

*Here's to living with our eyes wide open.*

# Table Of Contents

# FOREWORD

The idea for this pocketbook came to me during a pivotal time in my life – right after a layoff, during a season of redefining work and my new normal. I was in the process of building and growing my business, deciding whether I might re-enter the corporate world, and looking at my bank account to see what I could afford to do. I felt ready to leave my last company, but I wanted it to be on my terms, and I felt a sense of betrayal. I felt like a rug had been swept out from underneath me. Yet, I was also excited and focused on my business and having interesting conversations about a new world of possibilities.

People kept asking, "How are you?" I was feeling too much, too deeply, and it felt like too small of a question and too big of one all at once. Sometimes, that was acceptable – sometimes, it was not. So, I began responding with "I'm not really sure" because it seemed like the truest response to offer up in a moment.

One time, a friend asked me, and when I answered honestly, they responded with words that did not feel helpful, and I felt a little more unsettled and a little less hopeful. I understood their intent and recognized their love for me because of the depth of the relationship. And so, I stayed on the phone. What happened next was a miracle. They asked a different question: "Have you cooked anything lately you are really proud of or excited about?" And it made all the difference. Ironically, I had cooked something that I was super proud of. It was my first time making oxtails, and they were delicious. (I blended a baked sweet potato with the oxtail broth and created this sweet heat sauce to go over my heart of palm pasta. I am getting excited as I share this all over again.) I felt seen, and my entire countenance changed. Why? Everyone who knows me knows that I love exploring in my kitchen. It is a form of creative expression. I am good at it, and it is so good for my heart, mind, and soul. I had not shared my oxtail dish on social media, and this friend would have never known if she had not asked. Can you imagine what might have happened if my friend had led with this question?

That was the night that changed everything. I wanted to end the song and dance, and I started plotting "operation rage against the *how-are-you* machine."

The purpose of this book is to give permission to "askers" to ask a different, more meaningful question and for "responders" to give honest, meaningful answers (or decline to answer altogether). My hope is that you will be emboldened to try something new and experiment alongside me. I believe our relationships will be better for it.

# CHAPTER 1

# THE WHY

## Rethinking How We Engage

We've all had a conversation that starts like this:

Person 1: Hey, how are you?

Person 2: I'm good, how are you?

Person 1: I'm [insert okay, good, well, tired, taking it day by day… etc.].

End of conversation.

If you google "how are you" right now, you will get some interesting responses. I enjoyed the results that show how to ask *how-are-you* in other languages. I found quite a few sites explaining the purpose and use of *how-are-you* to non-American-English-speakers, such as YourDictionary, which defines *how-are-you* as an informal greeting not requiring a literal response. Another explainer site says *how-are-you* is simply another way to say hello. The results I found most relevant were articles like one in the Atlantic, titled "What to ask Instead of 'How Are You' During a Pandemic" and subtitled "Everyone's doing badly. We need better questions to ask."

We seem to be divided on our use of the question, with some not being bothered at all– responding with "good-tired-fine" over and over forever– and others feeling like it is a waste of a question. The introverts I know hate small talk, but I would not limit a disdain for *how-are-you* to just them from what I know about extroverts; the more shared, the merrier. I cannot pinpoint the preference to a particular group of individuals. However, the individuals reading this book make up the group of people who think, "we need better questions to ask."

If communication exists to further connection, *how-are-you* has completely missed the mark. You're here because this bothers you. You're tired of the monotony. You'd rather answer anything but that dreaded question. You've been a part of a conversation like that, and you'd rather not engage in one again. How-are-you feels too massive, yet so small. You crave depth and connection. Maybe you're here because you're curious (and that's ok, too). Perhaps you want to be a more interesting, engaging human who starts conversations with better questions. I'm here to show you that it is possible and how to start.

We ask *how-are-you* partly out of habit and expectation, partly out of convenience, and partly out of care. Most of us were taught to ask as kids or at least learned to model it based on adult interactions. The habit started at an early age. Expectation-wise, on one side of the coin, it's rude to start a conversation without inquiring. On the other side of that same coin, it's polite to ask. Asking *how-are-you* is so ingrained in us that we won't reflect on that part of the conversation unless...

1. We ask or are asked a different question or follow-up that demands more.

2. The person who answers chooses to answer the question in a way that matters and wakes you both up to life happening.

3. One person jumps into the conversation without inquiring about how you are at all!

Number 3 is considered a travesty. "How dare they go on without even considering whether I am okay or not?! Is their agenda more important than my existence? Oh, the drama that spirals from our minds down into our hearts when someone breaks an unwritten but very well-understood social contract. Whoever does not ask has told us they do not care about us.

Ironically, I believe the first *how-are-you* was grounded in care. The need to know that "you're ok, so I'm ok" confirms something more primitive-- our own safety. I believe we started asking *how-are-you* with the pure intention of exchanging stories. Storytelling is linked to our survival and evolution. It's what makes us human. I imagine the first *how-are-you* had more time attached to it-- enough time for the responder to tell a story and for the asker to share one back.

Fast forward to today, and we are all so distracted and itching to move on to the next thing on our agenda. We want what's convenient. It's not our fault—we have more going on than our ancestors did. We have access to too many stories—some that we never asked for or care to have access to: the work email and pings that sweep us into the next emergency, the text messages, the social media updates, stories, posts, or reels. Don't worry. This little book is not about being less distracted or less busy; there are plenty of other books on that. Before we dive into the alternatives to asking *how-are-you*, let us address mindset shifts through permission, choice, and action.

IT'S OKAY.

# CHAPTER 2

# A PAUSE FOR CHANGE

## Giving Yourself Permission to Break Conversation Norms

"Out with the old and in with the new" is a phrase that makes change seem like a nice, beautiful walk in the park. It leaves out the awareness needed and time to see the change. It leaves out the attachment, societal expectations, judgment, doubt, and awkwardness that come before deciding to make a change and going after it with all you've got.

Awareness is key, and I congratulate you for taking the first step. Maybe no one has told you lately, or ever, but you:

1. Can have great conversations without ever asking *how-are-you*. (You can totally skip the question altogether!)

2. Will not ruin a relationship if you respond to *how-are-you* in a way that honors where you actually are in the present moment.

You can do hard different things. I promise. I have practiced this myself. When I share my position on the question, people tend to do one of a few things. They will either:

- Be surprised by how you approach conversations.
- Question their relationship with *how-are-you*.
- Start asking you different questions or
- Continue asking *how-are-you*.

In case you're wondering, "What's the worst that could happen?" When I look at this list, the last point is truly the worst that has happened.

CHAPTER 3

# THE DARE TO BE DIFFERENT

## Making Bold Choices in Conversations

Our sameness is linked to survival, and that makes choosing a different approach a little scary. Sometimes we just need to hear that it is okay to be different and that we will be accepted for who we are in each moment. I invite you to be different. I invite you to be daring.

As a matter of fact, I dare you to be an asker who:

- **Remembers what people share of themselves with you**, even if it means taking notes.

- **Takes less offense** because humans will be human, and that leaves us open to being misunderstood.

- **Lets go of expectations** because others have freedom of choice just like you.

- **Makes an honest effort to commit** to starting a different conversation.

That's not all! I dare you to be a responder who:

- **Uses discernment and responds with tact**, respecting the person and situation.

- **Declines how-are-you** when you simply do not want to respond.

- **Assumes positive intent**, remembering that asking is vulnerable, too.

- **Strives for a balanced conversation** and asks a powerful question back.

Are you up for this challenge?

# CHAPTER 4

# SMALL SHIFTS, BIG ACTION

## Becoming the Change You Wish to See in Our World

In Chapter 1, I mentioned *how-are-you* as a habit. The great thing about habits is that they can be changed! If you desire to deepen your relationships, tell more interesting stories, or make different (read: better) connections, you may think it requires a massive personality shift or a major overhaul in how you communicate. Thankfully for you, this book is about changing one habit: asking a different question. As James Clear states in his book Atomic Habits, "It is so easy for us to overestimate the importance of one defining moment and underestimate the value of making small improvements on a daily basis. Too often, we convince ourselves that massive success requires massive action."

If you've ever thrown a pebble into a pond or played the telephone game, you've seen the effects of a 1-degree shift. The small but mighty pebble splashes and causes ripples in the water around it. The weight of the little pebble and the fact that it was thrown matters. The original message whispered into one person's ear is not the same message announced five whispers later. The speaking, hearing, listening, focus, and position of each player matter. There are a thousand metaphors on micro, repetitive change leading to massive, life-changing results for you to pick from. The point is to do the "small thing" for the opportunity to create lasting, positive effects in your life and the lives of others!

# A Moment of Science: Introducing Positive Psychology

(The purpose of this section is to give you a bit of science behind the why in case you need it to act. Permission to skip if nerding out is not your thing! )

As stated on positivepsychology.com, positive psychology is "a branch of psychology that studies the conditions that contribute to the optimal functioning of people, groups, and institutions." Simply stated, positive psychology is the study of human flourishing. In this chapter's context, the "small thing" of purposely asking a different question to deepen connection would be considered a positive psychology intervention, or PPI.

In her article on PPI, Madhuleena Chowdhury highlights the work of positive psychology researchers Sonja Lyubomirsky and Nancy Sin, who defined PPI as a psychological intervention that primarily focuses on raising positive feelings, thoughts, and behaviors. Chowdhury notes that all positive psychology interventions:

- Focus on enhancing happiness through positive thoughts and emotions and

- Sustain the effects long-term

Going one step further, Chowdhury notes that there are seven categories that PPIs fall into. This book highlights empathy-oriented positive interventions because its focus is on strengthening positive emotions in interpersonal relationships through effective communication.

(The field of positive psychology is a fascinating one, and this section barely covers the tip of the iceberg. Please look up the field and researchers mentioned in this section if you are interested in learning more.)

## Introducing the How Are You (H.A.Y.) Challenge

The next three chapters detail how to respond, how to frame questions, and the alternative options you have to replace how-are- you. Once you learn some alternative ways to ask and respond to *how-are-you*, you will have everything you need to engage in the H.A.Y. Challenge, where you refrain from asking *how-are-you* for a month. Below are the rules of engagement.

## Rule 1: Start

Start on the first day of the month because it will be easier for you to track.

### Rule 2: Do not H.A.Y. (AKA do not ask *how-are-you* for the month)

- If you H.A.Y., apologize and try again.

- If you mean *how-are-you* sincerely, ask "How are you, really?"

- If you don't want to know how a person is, own it internally, and DON'T H.A.Y. Instead, use an affirming statement like: "Hi, I'm looking forward to our convo" or "Hi, it's good to see you."

### Rule 3: Lean into different.

- Don't share that you are doing the H.A.Y. challenge with the people you are speaking to.

- Be open and honest with yourself and with others

### Rule 4: Do not use the How's-not-allowed listed below:

- How are you doing?
- How have you been?
- How's everything?
- How's it going?
- How are things going?
- What's going on?
- What's up / whassup?

**Rule 5: Take your pick of A-H.A.Y.s (alternative** *how-are-you*'s) **and choose your challenge.**

- Do feel free to pick a random one to try on for the day (that you ask everyone)

- See how many A-H.A.Y.s you can ask in one day (1 for each person you meet)

We spent the first half of this book focused on the who and why, and are just starting to get into the how. Buckle up, because this last half is where the magic action happens, and we are diving right in!

## CHAPTER 5

# **REAL TALK**

## Crafting Genuine and Authentic Responses

### How to Respond When You Do Not Want To

"No" and "Stop" are full-sentence boundary statements children learn early on. (Whether those boundaries are respected is a different book for another day.) While "No" and "Stop" still hold value, they are not appropriate responses to *how-are-you*. If you ever want to decline *how-are-you*, try responding with a version of the following:

- "Thank you for asking. I am not sure how I am doing or feeling at this moment."

- "I'd like to answer a different question" and proceed to share what you'd like to focus on

- "I have not taken the time to consider how I am doing lately, and need some time to reflect on that question"

- "I am not sure, but when I know I will get back to you"

- "How I am doing feels like a big question for me at this moment. I might be feeling overwhelmed."

Sometimes, connecting with other people in their lives helps us navigate what is coming up in our own. If you really want to take it to the next level, you can pass the baton back:

- "I need to warm up to that question. Are you open to sharing what is going on with you?"

## Responding With Honor & Grace

As you embark on responding truthfully, express gratitude towards the asker. Remember, in Chapter 1, we discussed how *how-are-you* comes from a genuine place, whether our current use of it is genuine in every situation. Always assume positive intent. Give grace to the asker and thank them for asking even when you choose not to answer.

While a big part of The H.A.Y. Challenge is not to share that you are completing a challenge, it is ok to share your "why" behind not wanting to answer the question. Your level of explanation and sharing may vary based on the depth of your relationship.

Additionally, you are the keeper of your relationships, and you know the people in your life best. To discern means to perceive or recognize. Discern which responses will both honor you and your truth in the moment as well as the person you are relaying or relating to.

## Literally, Don't Be Literal

There are times in passing when people say, "Hey, how are you" or "Hey, what's good." The how in the statement is not a question, and the expectation is to respond with "good, how are you" so that they can wrap up the greeting with "good" and move on.

"Hey, how are you" was a greeting statement and not the spark of a conversation. You were probably walking or in motion, and chances are they were doing the same. Do not, I repeat, do not make an awkward situation out of a greeting.

The way we give *how-are-you* back its power is by recognizing its use in different situations and changing our relationship with it. If someone greets you with *how-are-you* in passing, you still do not have to respond back with an equally passive "How are you?" Try one of these instead:

- Acknowledge + wish them well (e.g., Hey, have a great day)

- Acknowledge + affirm or compliment (Hey, I love your [hair, shoes, style, smile, etc.])

- Acknowledge + thank + wish them well (e.g., Hey, thank you, have a great day!)

You can bring conscientiousness into every conversation you choose to participate in. There is always a window of opportunity to wake someone up to their words and remind them of their humanity (and yours). If you really want to respond (because you can), keep it honest and short with a hey-hi-hello followed by your truth in the moment:

- I'm feeling tired today.
- I'm feeling sad.
- I am feeling great!

I believe people are grasping for connection without knowing it. In a world where everyone matters, the people in passing are no exception. People want to feel like they are good and altruistic. In your two seconds of honesty, you give the asker an opportunity to perform a spontaneous gesture of goodwill or to give.

Maybe they give you a smile, some words of wisdom, or a little encouragement for your day. According to the benefits of giving outlined in the Greater Good Magazine, when you allow someone the opportunity to give, you:

- Contribute to their happiness
- Increase their health
- Increase social connection in the world
- Evoke their sense of gratitude
- Create a ripple effect of giving

The last, but not least important action to take when responding: if you are able, look up and look the asker in the eye. Looking someone in the eye is an easy way to convey respect, understanding, and attention. If an asker did not want any part of that equation, I truly believe they would not have greeted you in the first place. The giving starts with you.

## You Ask, They Respond. Now What?

Most of this book is about the first exchange: what and how to ask and how to respond. However, it's important for askers to be aware of how they respond, especially if the responder has just shared vulnerably!

## Good Reports

How might you respond, if in response to your question, someone shares that they just got promoted, or engaged, or that some exciting life event has happened? According to Dr. Shelly Gable, a professor of psychology at the University of California, there are four ways to respond to good reports:

- **Active-constructive:** the responder is enthusiastic, interested and supportive. It might sound like, "That's exciting news! I'm so happy for you. How can I celebrate with or support you?" This is the best response—think of it as accepting the person's invitation to join them in their joy. See image below.

- **Passive-constructive:** the response is positive but short compared to the excitement of the sharer. *Think understated.* There is little to no additional inquiry. It might sound like, "That's nice" or "That's great," with no real interest or enthusiasm.

- **Active-destructive**: they belittle the good news or focus on the potential (yet non-existent in the moment) aspects of the good news. *Think: raining on a parade.* They might say, "Really, I heard morning sickness is a beast in the first trimester. It doesn't sound like a fun time to me."

- **Passive-destructive**: very little is said to acknowledge the good news. *Think: hijacking or ignoring.* The conversation is shifted to another topic or hijacked to be made about them. This might sound like, "Cool, what should we have for lunch?" or "It's great you got promoted. I was promoted two weeks ago."

|  | Constructive | Destructive |
|---|---|---|
| **Active** | Happy with | Unhappy with |
| **Passive** | Happy for | Unhappy for |

*Visual: Responding to Good Reports Active constructive responses are the best for increasing positivity and connection in relationships*

# CHAPTER 6

# THE ART OF INQUIRY

## Framing Questions for Meaningful Engagement

I am amazed by our human ability to do better once we know better and by how small tweaks can make a huge difference in how we experience the world.

This chapter might feel counterintuitive because our minds believe that bigger and more is better. However, the wealthiest and brightest people in this world understand the power of focus and the paradox of choice; more does not always mean better. In fact, according to the Design Lab, "an abundance of options actually requires more effort to choose and can leave us feeling unsatisfied with our choice."

If there are diminishing returns associated with more choices, and someone asks *how-are-you*, I would argue that for those of us who live dynamic lives, it's just too much for our brain to process and compare. When answering *how-are-you*, why wouldn't our brains default to giving a surface-level "good-fine-tired-okay" response? It saves time, energy, and effort. Our brains are not automatically incentivized to give more.

However, the more specific the ask, the fewer options we have in responding, the less filing our brains must do, and the more likely we are able to respond in a genuinely connective way. The following sections outline how to frame *how-are-you* using what, time, location/ place, and personal attributes. (This chapter lays the foundation. If you want to jump straight into practice, skip to Chapter 7 for alternative H.A.Y.s.)

## Using What to Frame

Consider turning your how question into a what question. For example, instead of asking how someone's weekend was, consider asking "what's one thing that brought you joy this weekend?" Additionally, instead of asking someone what they are excited about, consider asking "what's one thing you are looking forward to? You can help a person filter through all the things that might be swirling around in their minds. Your "what" question can help your responder focus and filter through all the things that might be swirling around in their minds because your question is pointed.

## Using Time to Frame

If we have not spoken in at least a month, *how-are-you* could cover every single day in the last month? If you are anything like me, I have been to too many places, seen too much, done too much, and felt too much to know how to answer that question.

On the other hand, if we speak every day or multiple times in a day, *how-are-you* at that frequency starts to rub up against the law of diminishing returns which states that benefits gained from something will represent a proportionally smaller gain as more energy is invested into it.

My favorite way to inquire *how-are-you* is to time-box it. For example, instead of asking, "How have you been" you might consider asking, "What's changed since we spoke last week?" or "What's one thing that brought you joy this weekend?"

## Using Location & Place to Frame

What happens when we run on autopilot? The simple things get taken for granted. We forget to notice the world around us. When we are busy not-noticing, we miss the sweetness of the moment. Sometimes that sweetness is an activation of the senses. Sometimes the sweetness is a funny people-watching moment. Most times, the sweetness is grounding and getting out of our heads. What might it look like to ask *how-are-you* in a way that brings a person back to the present? What a gift it is to help those around us notice the goodness right in front of them!

I know the weather conversation might feel old for those who experience work in the corporate world like I do, but we have it because many of us can relate to enjoying sunny days and the yearning to go outside. Where we are has an impact on how we feel. Consider asking others to explore the weather, the music that's playing in the background, and what's happening where they are in this very moment.

## Using Personal Attributes to Frame

How-are-you is a generic question that can be asked to anyone, and that is why it is asked to everyone by everyone. We are an adaptive species, wired to get things done quickly and efficiently to conserve energy. I won't knock the greatest machine ever created! Here is another fact about our brains—we have a need to feel significant (i.e., unique and special). In his article, "The Science of Mattering: Why Feeling Significant is So Significant," Dr. Zach Mecurio states, "Feeling significant is found to increase serotonin levels, sometimes called the "confidence molecule" that influences overall mood and lowers anxiety." He adds that "mattering also reaffirms that we contribute to others and that we have a purpose." In a world where everyone wants to feel special, why not help them?

The hardest part about asking *how-are-you* in a way that helps someone feel special and cared for is that… you have to care and believe they are special. Most of the time, when we care, we remember. I believe we care about humans on a micro and macro level. The micro level is easy because it means caring about an individual based on an existing relationship or being invested in the potential for a future relationship.

Macro-caring, as you probably guessed, is being fascinated by humanity and genuinely curious about the story each person has to tell. I liken it to having a God-view of how valuable and special each person on this Earth is. Someone who has made a life around this is Brandon Stanton, creator of Humans of New York (HONY). HONY is a book of street portraits and interviews Brandon started over ten years ago. His level of curiosity and care for humanity has reached millions of people.

While I mentioned micro-level-caring is easy, it does not mean macro-level-caring hard. It does, however, require intentionality. For example, if you have a hard time remembering names, you can tie a person's name with a unique fact about them. Then, the next time you meet them, your how-are- you replacement question can reference that unique fact. Even if you forget their name, they will be delighted that you remembered something special about them. How awesome!

## Bringing it All Together

You can use multiple frames at once! Do you remember the story in the beginning of this book when I mentioned the question my friend asked me about cooking? If not, that's okay. Consider this modified example using three of the four framing techniques: "What's one dish you cooked in the last month that you are really proud of?" This question:

- Starts with what and asks the responder to focus on one

- Specifies a time frame of one month

- Is specific to a person who likes to cook

Location is a bonus. While not explicitly stated, it is implied that the person cooks at home 99% of the time!

While the frames were broken down a bit methodically in this chapter, the key takeaway is to be present and intentional in your asking. As you dive into the many questions you have at your disposal in Chapter 7, see if you can notice where some of the frames show up.

# A WORLD OF QUESTIONS

## Diversifying Your Conversational Toolkit

The moment you've been waiting for: what to ask if you won't be asking *how-are-you*. In this chapter, you will find different questions to ask based on time, situation, person, and place, as well as the context for why or how they work.

## When the Person is in a Different Location from You

- Where in the world are you joining/calling in from today? They may have a story to share. You may have been there before, and now there is a point of connection.

- What's the weather like where you are? Studies show that weather affects our mood. The responder may also share their sentiment about the weather.

## When You Are In The Same City

- How are you enjoying/ how have you enjoyed the weather today? This is a great question to ask mid-day, especially on a sunny day. If the responder has not been outside, this is a great prompt for them to go.

- Have you been anywhere today that you'd recommend I go? This is a great one if you are visiting a city. It allows you an opportunity to learn what the responder enjoys getting into and offers the asker an adventure!

## When You Don't Know Anyone

I love these for networking events or any group events with strangers. Most likely, the responders will have a story.

- Is this your first time?

- Have you been here before?

- What brings you here today?

- How did you find out about this event?

## When You Speak On A Cadence: Daily, Weekly, Or Monthly

- What's new since we last spoke? It's time-boxed! This is a great question for responders who always seem to have so much happening. Even if the responder can't think of one new thing at the moment, they will!

- What's one thing that brought you joy today/ this week/ this month? This is a great life-pulse-check question. Be prepared to have your answer in case the responder needs more time to respond.

## When It Has Been Awhile (Like Years)

If you come across someone you have not seen in awhile, the truth is you probably do not want to know how they are feeling right now right away. You probably want to know how they have been in the gap since you last saw each other! Why? Because that's a story, and stories make life interesting!

If you are talking to them, I assume you know them well enough to consider a conversation after so much time has passed. If you have not seen this person in a while, the assumption is that you do not know what is going on in their life. Even if you follow them on social media, you do not really know, so I encourage you to test it.

- Wow, It's been so long. I don't even know where to start! Sometimes you need to start here while the shock wears off.

- I remember the last time we met, you were [insert activity]. Are you still [insert activity]?

- Where do you live now/ where are you based now?

- I saw you were [insert activity, location, etc.] on [insert social media platform]. How was that?

## Depending On The Day Of The Week

This section assumes a typical work week with 4-5 days working and 2-3 days not working.

### Going into the weekend

- How was your work week? Avoid this question if you know the person does not like their job. It's the quickest way to a negative mood that can be avoided! Consider "Is there anything you'd like to share about your work week" or better yet…

- Do you have rest or play planned for this weekend?

*Going into the work week*

- How have you been preparing for the work week?

- Do you feel rested going into the next work week?

## Depending On The Time Of Day

These questions allow the responder to take stock of their day.

### Morning

- What's one thing you are looking forward to today? If they cannot think of anything, you've just created space for them to create their own positive intervention. The great thing about the morning-- they have the rest of the day!

### Midday

- What's today been like for you so far? Consider the person you are asking and the situation. If you are in a time-boxed business meeting, and you know this person loves providing detail, consider asking a different question!

### End of the day

- What's one thing that sparked joy for you today? This is one of my favorite questions. We cannot expect constant happiness, but we can create opportunities for experiencing joy.

## Around Mealtime

Skipping meals contributes to low blood sugar. Low blood sugar can cause irritability, moodiness, headaches, and feelings of tiredness.

- Did you have breakfast this morning?

- Have you had lunch or dinner yet?

## When You Sense Transition

- Where are you coming from? This question creates space for acknowledgement and pause. I enjoy using it when I notice someone seems hurried or rushed. When that happens, I allow them to take a breath (or a few).

## When You Sense The Person Seems "Down" Or "Off"

We generally stay away from closed questions that solicit yes or no responses. However, I've found that if I sense properly, this response is never just a "yes" or a "no." Sometimes. people respond with "Yes, why?" and that leads us down a path. Other times, it's a "no, thank you for asking," or "no, how could you tell" or "no, but I don't want to talk about it."

- Are you ok?

- Are you feeling okay today?

## During A Tough Time

Be sure to acknowledge the "thing" by saying, "Hi, I understand you are going through a tough time." If the situation was recently shared, say, "Thank you for sharing what is happening," and ask:

- What's coming up for you?

- How have you been reflecting?

- Have you had a chance to mourn/grieve?

- Is there anything I should/could be asking you that I am not?

## When a Loved One is in the Hospital

You may have a loved one in the hospital or know someone who has a loved one in the hospital. These questions work either way.

- How have you been sleeping?

- How is your appetite?

- How are the nurses/doctors treating you (patient) or how are the nurses/doctors communicating with you (supporter of patient)?

- I'd like to come support/visit. Is that ok?

- Is there anything I can bring you?

- I want to pray for you. What are you hoping for?

## During Exciting Times

Exciting times may include a victorious season, an accomplishment, or an event. Always express gratitude: "Wow, thank you for sharing this moment with me." Also, be ok with them celebrating... or not!

- What are you most proud of? This is wonderful question for responders to go reflect on and appreciate the work of their hands.

- Is your cup full or empty? Sometimes, celebratory events deplete us, like huge parties.

- What was the process like?

- Would you do it all over again? This may have been a once-in-a-lifetime celebration, don't you want in on that?

- Did you enjoy it, and would you recommend it?

- Have you celebrated yet?

- How will you celebrate if you have not already?

## On A Birthday Or Anniversary:

- What makes this day special for you? The answer to this question might surprise you!

- How do you or would you like to be celebrated? Another one of my favorite questions because not many people ask!

- What's your favorite memory of this special day? Have you ever noticed the glimmer in a person's eyes when they recall a really good time in their life?!

- What do you wish (or pray) for? This is a great way to learn something new and important about a person that they may not have shared otherwise.

## When You Know What Sparks Joy For A Person

These questions will vary depending on the person and your depth of knowledge for them. The important part is knowing the person and being considerate and creative!

- What's the last dish you made?
- Have you read any juicy books lately?
- How was your game last week?

…and the list goes on! Think of 5 people you know well and what brings them joy. Using the space below, write down their names, what you know about them, and the alternative H.A.Y. you plan on asking the next time you connect with them.

| Name | Job-Bringing-Thing | Your Creative Question |
|------|--------------------|-----------------------|
| ① _____ | _____ | _____ |
| ② _____ | _____ | _____ |
| ③ _____ | _____ | _____ |
| ④ _____ | _____ | _____ |
| ⑤ _____ | _____ | _____ |

## When You Don't Want to Ask, State

Remember earlier on when I mentioned that it's ok not to ask? Maybe you do not have the time or energy to go deep in the moment. Maybe you do not care to know. (Let's be honest.) If you are in a situation where genuinely asking an Alternative H.A.Y. is not an option, skip it and take the following steps instead:

1. **Notice.** Take in your environment and the person.

2. **Make a positive statement.** You may want to assume "give a compliment" and that is exactly why step 2 does not say that. A positive statement could be:

   a. Giving them a direct compliment

   b. Stating how you are looking forward to your time together

c. Expressing positive emotion about your (shared) surroundings

3. **Give space for response.** Allow them a moment to agree or say thank you.

4. **Move on.**

## Over Text

There is something lovely about being thought of and told that you've been thought of. I have often found that sharing one of the below generally leads to the receiver sharing how they're doing, without me asking. Integrity matters, so be sure to only use it if the statement is true for you!

- You were on my mind
- Checking in/ checking on you
- Thinking of you/ thought of you
- Just prayed for you
- I am looking forward to connecting with you
- Would you like to do (or go to) ____ [insert place or activity] with me?

## Based on Social Styles (for Business)

The Social Styles Model focuses on outer behavior–how individuals communicate– based on a set of personality characteristics. While I learned this model in the corporate consulting world, I have witnessed its power in any business setting. It is an amazing tool for best understanding how to communicate with clients, managers, and coworkers. There are four social styles: analytical, amiable, driver, and expressive. While I am only covering things to consider for each style, I highly recommend looking into the Social Styles if you work in a business setting.

## Analytical & Driving

These 2 styles control emotion and will want to get to the agenda or point of the conversation faster

- Those with analytical style may ask a how- are-you question and dig deeper into your response, but may give a very short response when asked the same question. Tip: Be okay with answering how you are first, and then inquiring about them as the conversation goes on. Expect them to ask follow up questions to your answer as they tend to like depth of knowledge.

- Those with driving style may dive straight into their agenda without asking a *how-are-you* question at all. They may even seem bothered by the question or response if it is considered too "fluffy" or "flowery." Tip: Keep it brief with "it's good to see you" and ask "what's on your agenda for today"Enter the conversation ready to tackle the task or agenda at hand.

## Expressive & Amiable

These two styles display emotion and focus on feelings and relationships. They will want to talk and or hear how people are feeling/doing.

- Those with expressive style may be very excited to share how they feel when asked. So much so, that it takes up more of the conversation than planned. In fact, they may not even need to be asked at all. Tip: Send an agenda before the meeting if you have one. If you use PowerPoint, and you are meeting virtually, pull up the agenda early on in the conversation and anchor there. Consider starting the conversation with "it's good to see you" and saying you are excited to talk about [insert agenda items here] if you are short on time. Or, after it's good to see you, ask a limited question like "what's one thing you are looking forward to today?" Lastly, if you are in charge of the agenda, consider baking in additional time for catching up or exchanging pleasantries – that way you are not rushing a colleague or client!

- Those with amiable style may spend the entire meeting listening to you and trying to figure out how they can support you because they care.

However, they may do this without getting to the planned agenda, causing delays for them, the team and or the projects they are responsible for. Tip: If you want to know how an individual with an amiable style is feeling, you may want to ask the "how are you, really" question. You may also want to start with "It's good to see you, and I look forward to hearing what you had in mind for us to talk about/cover today."

## Based on Love Languages

The questions in this section allow people to do their own reflection on whether their love tank has been filled or not. Their responses allow you to fill it up a little more! I only recommend asking these questions to those you are in an intimate-enough-relationship with to know their love language. Additionally, you might want to say, "I know your love language is [insert love language]", and then ask the question. Prefacing the question lets people know you are being intentional in the moment!

### Acts of Service

- What's on your to-do list/agenda for today?

- What have you been working on?

### *Receiving Gifts*

- Have you received anything lately that made you feel seen?

### *Quality Time*

- What's one thing you've spent time doing today that's sparked love, peace, or joy?

### *Physical Touch*

- Has anyone hugged you today?

### *Words of Affirmation*

- Have you received any compliments yet today?
- Has anyone said anything nice to you yet today?

Lastly, consider whether you can and are willing to fill their love tank. For example, if their love language is physical touch, and you ask them if they have received a hug today, and they say no, be prepared to gift them a hug! If they have not received a compliment, do not leave them empty-handed. Be prepared to love them well. Otherwise, you are not stewarding well.

## Based on VIA strengths:

The VIA (Values in Action) Inventory of Strengths is an assessment designed to identify an individual's profile of positive character strengths. You can find some potential questions below for seventeen of the twenty-four strengths. (A full list of the VIA Strengths is available online.) Much like the love languages, I would only ask these questions if you know the other person's VIA Strengths. I would preface the question with, "I remember one of your strengths is [insert strength]...

## Appreciation of Beauty or Excellence

- Have you experienced anything inspiring in the past [insert time, since we last met]

## Bravery

- Have any situations called you to be brave today?
- When was the last time you did something that scared you?

## Creativity

- Have you created anything recently that you were proud of, and did you share it with anyone?

## Curiosity

- What's the last thing that fed your curiosity?
- Have you gone on any wild searches for information recently?
- Where has your curiosity taken you since the last time we connected?

### Fairness

- I saw [insert event] on the news/social media. What are your thoughts on the situation?

### Gratitude

- What's one thing you are grateful for today?

### Hope

- What's one thing you are hoping for in this conversation?
- What's one thing you are hoping for this week/month/year?

### Humor

- I could use a good laugh—got any good jokes on hand?
- What's the last thing that made you laugh?

### Judgment

- I am in the process of making a decision. What are your thoughts?

### Kindness

- Have you participated in or witnessed any acts of kindness that made your heart smile?

### Love of Learning

- What's the last fun fact you learned?
- What are you studying right now?
- What's the last thing you read, and what did you learn from it?

### Perseverance

- What's one challenge you've faced this week, and how did you overcome it?

### Perspective

- [Insert problem or situation.] What's your take?

### Prudence

- What might you do to prevent [insert situation] from happening?

### Self-regulation

- What's your morning routine?
- What's one habit you created that you've found beneficial?

### Social Intelligence

- Have you had the opportunity to reflect on [insert circumstance]?

*Spirituality*

- What are you praying for?

## A Word on Models & Tools

You can ask powerful *how-are-you* alternatives regardless of the model. These tools were created for a better understanding of self and others. There are so many individual and group "typing" tools out there! The ones you know of will vary based on your exposure and interest in them. The only requirement is to be specific to the individual and ask according to their "thing," whether that's Meyers Briggs, Enneagram, Gallup Strengths, VIA Strengths, Love Languages and so on!

# CHAPTER 8

# CONNECTION STARTS WITH YOU

## Exploring Options for Daily Positivity Practice

Our awareness of and connection with others often re-flects how aware and connected we are with ourselves. Maybe this day or that day just was not your day. That is okay. Chapter 5 covered how to respond when you do not know how you are doing or feeling in the moment.

What if there were ways to know? What if there were little things you could do to spark joy in a pinch, so you always had a response to an asker's attempt at connecting with you?

The following activities help me savor the sweetness in each day.

## Three Good Things

Martin Seligman, the father of positive psychology, found that writing three "good things" and your contribution to making each of the good things happen significantly increased happiness and decreased depressive symptoms immediately after the exercise.

## Prayer and Thanksgiving

If you are a person of faith like me, keeping a prayer journal and praying the ACTS prayer (adoration, confession, thanksgiving, supplication) increases my positivity. My celebration and gratitude jar also helps. It has been fun to watch the jar fill up with notes that represent goodness in my life!

## Lean into Learning

Adopt a growth (versus fixed) mindset where you learn from your experiences, ask questions, and embrace the challenges that come with being alive.

### Remember (Your) Humanity

There are so many aspects of being human that social media has taught us to ignore or to pretend do not exist. We do not get to escape the human experience of shame, hurt, and frustration. The world becomes a brighter, more vivid place the moment we accept this truth for ourselves and others.

### Notice

Appreciate the world via your senses. If you are able, smell the roses. Look up at the sky and the trees. Savor the food you taste. Get carried away by a song. Feel the breeze or sun upon your face. Breathe with intention.

Then, when it's all said and done and someone asks you *how-are-you* or the alternative, think about these things and share!

# CHALLENGE COMMITMENT

I commit to using Alternative H.A.Y.s for the month of _____, 20___ [ Insert month and year]

During this time, I will either [select one method]:

☐ Use the same Alternative H.A.Y. all month.

☐ Rotate between 2-5 Alternative H.A.Y.s of my choice, listed below:

- _____
- _____
- _____
- _____
- _____

## Join the Movement

You will never be in this challenge alone, as it is my daily practice. If you are the type of person that likes to "seal the deal" and take actio n in the community, you can do this by scanning the QR code image below or visiting the website: beyondhowareyou.com. While this is an additional support mechanism, it is completely okay to continue reading the book without signing up. You may not need or want to, and you're still a part of this good work either way!

# ABOUT THE AUTHOR

Alexandria Theresa Skeete, a child of God, engineer by education, and strategist by trade, has been a thinker and writer for as long as she can remember. As a positive psychology practitioner, she is fascinated by all things wellness and human flourishing. Her happy place is creating safe spaces for greater understanding, depth, and connection.

Alexandria is on a mission to create more than she consumes, and this book is only a small reflection of that.

For holding this book in your hands, she offers her deepest gratitude.

If you would like to connect with or work with Alexandria, visit her website: alexandriatheresa.com or scan the QR code below.

www.livelifehappypublishing.com

www.ingramcontent.com/pod-product-compliance
Lightning Source LLC
Chambersburg PA
CBHW011218120626
46545CB00008B/3047

* 9 7 8 1 9 9 0 4 6 1 5 5 2 *